WINNING WAYS OF
MODERN PIGEON RACING

By CHARLES W. LYONS

(SEALION)

FOURTH EDITION

WINNING WAYS OF
MODERN PIGEON RACING

By
C. W. Lyons

FOREWORD

To justify myself in writing this book on the sport of long distance pigeon racing, I think I shall have to do the same as a well-known racehorse tipster did when offering his tips to the public. No doubt many of you will have met this gentleman in market places or outside the northern racecourses, who launches off like this:— " Gentlemen, if you wish to be guided on matters of the turf, i.e., the glorious and gentlemanly sport of horse-racing, then I am a fit and proper person to guide you, because in the first place, I served seven years in that well-known and most dangerous stable, Alex— of Manton. Do I know what a racehorse is, do I ? Well, I have ridden So and So," and so on he goes until he thinks he has convinced his audience that he is " that fit and proper person " to guide them and pick out the winners for them.

I think I ought to tell you something of my apprentice-ship amongst the pigeon fanciers of the " Old School," and believe me, the game then did not lack excitement. I well remember one little incident of the " catch and show " era of pigeon racing—the year was 1885, two years before the Jubilee of the late Queen Victoria. Birds had to be caught and taken to the appointed public-house for vertification. First in won. On this particular occasion I had to run my dad's pigeon in when it came, but some men in the race engaged professional runners to do this. My dad's racer arrived, and it was given to me in a black cloth bag. Away I went at full speed to the public-house, which was situated in a particularly long street, at the corner of an off side street. The " pub " had its usual double swing doors at the corner, and I was making for the side entrance just as a profes-sional runner came into view from the other end racing

like a deer. I looked like being beaten on the post when
one of the crowd waiting slipped inside the " pub " and
put the bar across the swing doors. The crowd was
shouting words of encouragement to me, naturally, a kid
against a man, but with a great burst of speed, my
opponent dashed at the swing doors, only to be hurled
back almost unconscious. The doors were unbolted
quickly and the crowd tried to make him believe that he
had struck the corner of the building instead. We won,
but for years after, that incident and many others of the
" old school of spin for the road and distance," rankled
in my mind. To-day, however, thanks to the gentlemen
who founded the National Homing Union—with special
mention for that grand old stalwart, George Yates, to
whom the sport owes much—it has been made fit for kings
and to any young man or even old. I can recommend
it as a good clean sport, in fact, second to none.

Well, when I grew up, I was very lucky among the
short distance men, but more often than not when one had
been successful with a good pigeon once or twice, it was
barred from certain races. All this tended to give me a
hankering after the long distance pigeon racing. This I
joined after returning from the Boer War in 1902. Mention of the Boer War brings to mind a little episode of
what British Tommies with the pigeon flying instinct
would do. We had been on Blockhouse duty for some
weeks, which was getting very monotonous. One night
our sentry was hidden behind a " sangar " (a breastwork
of stones) when an old white-faced Veldt cow popped its
head over the top. Billy, the sentry, promptly conked
out, thinking, as he said afterwards, that it was a ghost.
The next day Billy had a bad head and dysentery, so we
took him out in the open air and sat him on an old empty
biscuit box. He had not been sat there many minutes
before we saw him leap into the air and come back yelling
like " Hell." He had cause to do, as the box had become
the home of a nest of hornets and some of them had crept
under his shirt. Poor Billy, the blisters were like duck

eggs, and our only remedy rifle oil, but luckily the armoured train came along an hour later and took him to hospital.

After he had gone, the six of us left emptied some cartridges of cordite, and went down to the hornets' nest to smoke them out. An inspiration came to one of the boys; we picked six of the unconscious hornets up and marked dots on the wings with an indelible pencil, then putting them into a glass pickle-jar, we awaited their revival. We organised a race of a mile, and the " kitty " was a ticky each (3d.). Two went off with the hornets, which were duly liberated and, believe me, the one marked with six dots was the first to drop on the biscuit box, being duly swatted and taken to the Blockhouse for verification. I was the winner. This nest of hornets gave us many a break during our tedious and lonely vigil on the Veldt, and when we left we passed them over, to our relief, with all due ceremony.

Having introduced myself with these little stories, I wish to say that I flew pigeons in all classes of clubs until the Great War, joining up in 1914. After the finish I took up pigeon racing on a much bigger scale than I had been able to before and flew successfully up to 1935. I visited many of the great home lofts and also the best lofts in Belgium. I was always interested in the types and strains of pigeons, but more so in systems of training, feeding and foods, also loft accommodation, etc., after a careful study of which I came to the conclusion that it is the man who makes good birds give of their best. What I mean to infer to the beginner or novice is that a good bird cannot give of its best unless properly treated, and if you are not prepared to look after and properly tend your pigeons, it is a waste of money to buy classical racing birds.

WINNING WAYS OF MODERN PIGEON RACING.

CHAPTER I.

THE first thing the beginner should do is to think and reckon up how much of his pocket-money can be spared for his pigeons, always bearing in mind the good old Yorkshire motto, " Let your pocket be your guide, your eyes be your judge, and your money the last thing you part with." Now, before obtaining the birds, buy or build a loft, the size of which should be to hold about six to eight pairs more than you have decided to keep and make sure that the loft will not be an eyesore to your neighbours. It does not need to be elaborate or fancy, just a lean-to type sloping from back to front. You should be able to reach the roof inside comfortably with your hand. Birds get too wild if they are able to fly over your head in the loft. Trapping arrangements and all fittings should be decided upon after paying a visit to one or two lofts, and then if you have ideas of your own, try them out in your new loft.

Pigeon fanciers have a lot to blame themselves for when they get antagonistic with their neighbours—I will quote a few " Do nots " at this point. If you reside on a Council estate, do not disobey the Council's rules and regulations. It is your good conduct on these estates that gives you the privilege of keeping racing pigeons, that might also influence other Councils to give similar sanction and favours to would-be fanciers on their estates.

Unless your loft is on an allotment or field or well away from house property, **do not** give your birds " **free hole.**" On the wing or in the loft should be the motto. There are so many mistaken ideas as to the damage pigeons can do to house property, that it is not worth the risk of argument, especially with people already preju-diced. **Do not** allow your scrapings from the loft to lie about, as flies are apt to gather. Do not start to scrape the loft out in the wee small hours when your neighbours have another hour or so to rest. Be reasonable in all things. When your neighbour's cat begins to trouble you

and your birds, do not start shouting and creating about
it. Get one or two shallow trays, putting about half an
inch deep of creosote oil in them, and if a loose board
happens to be on the edge of the loft or other place where
pussy promenades, he might accidentally drop into the
tray. When he goes home and spoils one or two cushions,
he may have to be sent to a cats' home; in fact he will
have lost his owner's warm heart due to his pocket being
touched possibly for new covers or carpets. Anyhow, the
cure is certain. **Do not** throw stones or garbage at your
birds when on the house-top. If they have the habit of
dropping there, get a cord fixed to the chimney breast and
half-way down the roof fix a tennis ball to same. The
other end can hang on a hook on the loft, and when the
birds try to drop give the cord a swing upwards—the ball
will do the rest. If your neighbour asks whether you can
put silencers on your pigeons during the " wee small "
hours, do not show temper, just politely tell him that the
R.S.P.C.A. would not allow you to do so, but the next
time he has to get up in the " wee small " hours to help
his wife with the carpet beating, ask him to give you a
call, when you will lend him your silent vacuum cleaner.
ALWAYS BE POLITE! Anyhow, as we go on I might
find a few more " Do nots," this being from the pen of
a fancier who has had a lot to put up with re neighbours.

CHAPTER II.

Now we will take it that the Autumn is the best time to
start a loft, being the time of the year when fanciers have
a few good birds for disposal. The clearance auction
sales are also on, and a visit to these will be very instruc-
tive. Stand by and listen to one or two of the old hands
when they are handling and criticising any of the pigeons
for sale; you will hear much that will be beneficial in the
future. Fanciers of all kinds will be there, ready to offer
the beginner good advice, and if of the listening type, you
will surely learn. When buying birds, do not purchase
from a loft that is too far away from your own. After

getting established, then you may, if you wish, go further afield to find fresh blood, but if possible, secure your racers from fanciers situated between your loft and the first racepoint. As a beginner, you will do better if you place yourself in the hands of some good and successful fancier to guide you in the selection of stock. Personally I should advise you to purchase some well grown late breds from parents that have flown well during the previous racing season. Of course, you will have to take the risk of sex up to a point; some late bred birds are easy to tell, others are not until the following Spring.   In buying these late breds it will do away with the necessity of breaking off older birds.

Now, about the strain of birds to choose. Some strains do better in one fancier's hands than another, but you can take it, generally, that there are " good uns " and " bad uns " in all strains or families of pigeons.   I advocate the choosing of two strains from two different successful racing lofts.   Keep two or three pairs pure and make up a couple of crossed pairs. You will need to watch these late breds during the winter. Feed them well and see that they get no check in their growth, otherwise if they get a real setback you will have to kill them.

The Moult.

This is the annual event for the re-clothing of all the feathered tribe by Mother Nature, and birds living under natural conditions seem to get through this period without any setbacks or trouble. Birds, and especially pigeons, being kept under what we might term artificial conditions need to have a sharp eye kept on them during this period for any check or accident to the feathers that may cause blood quills to form in the wing. These blood quills are sometimes caused through malnutrition, and they are at most times a difficult problem to deal with, but on no account must they be pulled out. It would lead in most cases to further rupturing the folicle or seat of the quill, and only grow a worse feather the next time. It should be held daily under the cold water tap, and a capsule or two each day of halibut liver oil given to the subject. When a check occurs it shows by frets in the flights and sheathed neck or tail feathers. Treat as for blood quills, but the greatest thing of all is to keep the loft a normal temperature at nights. **Do not** leave your lofts with open fronts at night-time during the moult. Have shutters fixed or tack some old corn sacks up over your dowelled fronts.

You see our so changeable climate, especially at night, is bad for the birds during the moult and just at the time when you want those last two end flights to grow so well. At this time of the year your birds have to be fed early, and perhaps your feeding is not conducive to help very much in growing the right kind of feather, and perhaps their last feed has passed through them before midnight. Consequently they have not sufficient nourishment in their bodies to give them bodily heat, let alone a surplus of this nourishment to grow the young feathers that are struggling through. Keep the loft warm until the moult is through, then gradually drop your shutters and feed ordinary mixtures as you fancy. The moult starts just when the corn is being harvested and the wild herbs and grasses are shedding their seeds. These soon sprout and also the oats and wheat sheddings on the stubble. Our wild friends make good use of these, and see the amount of fat the wild birds accumulate as well as going through the moult. The mixture for the moult is given with corn recipes.

CHAPTER III.

TAKING it for granted that you have wintered your birds well, you should put them on a good diet for a week or two before pairing up. This is quite necessary, because the pairing and breeding—with the consequent excitement and rearing of youngsters—takes a lot out of the parents, and if not in real good condition at the start, you are going to have weakly youngsters as well as old ones unfit to race. **Do not** be impatient and pair up too soon. For late breds the end of April will be early enough, for other

yearlings the second week in March and for stock birds
the end of February, that is, if you fancy early youngsters
and are willing to take the chance. I do not advise this
early pairing, as the risk, feeding expense, and time are
more than what I think these youngsters would be worth.
Unless you are contemplating trying two or three young
cocks out on the " jealousy system," then earlier the
better. Of course, there are odd exceptions now and
again, but these do not justify the indiscriminate breeding
of early birds, until you have had a season or two's
experience. You must bear in mind that you are taking
something out of the old birds they can ill afford to spare
in the early part of the year, and in a climate like ours this
is a lot. The successful breeder is the one who is patient
and thinks things well over before doing anything about
the loft.

Now at this stage you must get your stud book and
enter up intended pairs (these should have been thought
out and paired on paper during the winter months) under
the nest box numbers you are going to allot them.

Nest Boxes.—My favourite nest box is one where the
nest front lies four or five inches back ; this leaves a box
perch for the bird on the outside. The entrance in the
nest front will be at the bottom and a bolting wire fixed.
The great idea of having the entrance on the floor of the
nest box is, that when a cock is driving hard it will save
him knocking himself about—you can fasten his hen up in
the box by fixing the bolting wire. The cock is then able
to play and bill with the hen without going to the extreme
and chasing her all over the place. The second benefit
from this nest box is that if a youngster gets into the
wrong box, it can get out quickly before being scalped.
You will notice that the majority of scalped youngsters
you come across are from lofts where the entrance is in
the middle of the nest front, and a strange one is not
quick enough to find it, before the old inmates of the box
are after its blood for intruding. Then again, you can
keep the cock or hen—whichever it is—in while its mate

is away at the race, and it will not be annoying the other occupants of the loft by wandering into this and that nest box. VERY IMPORTANT:—Feeding pots for nest boxes—these are a real necessity, and the **best yet** you generally have in the house and do not know it. It is the one pound glass jam jar. Get a piece of cardboard, stand the jar on it, then mark round it with a pencil, and cut out inside the circle. Fill the jar half full of sand, put in the cardboard disc, and press firmly down. Being glass, you are able to see when the jar requires refilling.

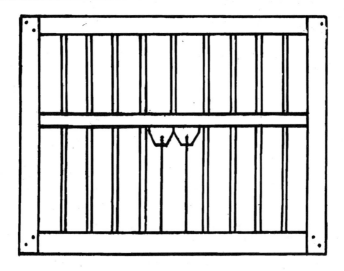

BOLTING WIRE FASTENER

NATURAL SYSTEM NEST FRONT

Frame, 1½-in. x ⅞-in. Middle Bar, 1-in. x ⅞-in. ¾-in. Dowells. Rustless Aluminium Bolting Wires are the best and lightest. Ordinary size Tea Chests with the above Front set 5 or 6 inches back makes an ideal Nest Box.

CHAPTER IV.

You must be ever watchful for sulky hens now you have put up the pairs as required. **Do not** get into that careless or carefree way of thinking they will come to. They will, no doubt, but what a gruelling before settling down. Take them out and let each occupy the box alternately, the other flying about the loft on its own. Seeing others settling down to their domestic duties will soon have the desired effect. Nesting material—a little sawdust or sand mixed with a little salt in the bottom of the nest-pan. You will never be troubled with red mite or any kind of ticks. Salt is the finest thing in the world for the destruction of blood sucking parasites. Also put some chopped straw in.

Now, when you think they are all nicely paired up, you will have to let them out of their boxes, one or two pairs at a time. After a while, get them back into the boxes and let another couple of pairs out.

This you must do until they know their own boxes quite well. Some fanciers paint the nest fronts alternately different colours. This, no doubt, helps the birds a good deal. At the end of seven or eight days the hens should be getting down on eggs which should be booked up as laid. During incubation go about the loft just ordinarily, not creeping about. Once and for all, **be your natural self,** but do not at any time make sudden loud noises that will startle the birds. Now is the time to add a little salt to the drinking water, also sprinkle a little amongst the grit. The amount should be one dessertspoonful of salt to a gallon of water. At the end of seventeen days from the second egg you should be looking or listening out for youngsters in the nest. I will not go into the question of feeding at this point—you will find a chapter on this and foods further on. If you are a fancier who has to be out early to his job and not much time to spare in the morning, this is where the glass feeding jars come in. These can be filled the previous evening, also the water pot. In the morning a sharp look round, then let the birds out for exercise and get the wife or someone else to see them in. On returning in the evening scrape out your loft—not having had time in the morning—**do this before letting out the birds for exercise.** Get them used to this loft scraping, it will help them to tame down a lot. Do this daily, and while you are about the loft or taking a quiet smoke, cast your eyes over the youngsters. If you hear any kind of plaintive squeaking coming from any of them, see what is wrong. You might possibly find the nest pan surrounded by a soft frothy excrement, in which case get the youngsters out and destroy them; or it may be canker in the throat. Give the bird a light squeeze with finger and thumb, and if the lump does not disappear, well destroy it. Inspect the old birds and give them a dose of Epsom Salts and a blood pill or two before letting them go to nest again. Put a mark against them to remind you to give special observation to their next youngsters. If these turn out like the previous ones, and other youngsters in the loft are doing well, you must separate the parents to try and find out with which lies the fault. **When this is done you should kill it.**

Never try to rear a sickly youngster, it does not pay. A pigeon's life is a very hard one, and therefore he must start from " scratch " as an A1 grade specimen. Pedigree is usually the excuse for rearing, but when a youngster leaves the nest box with a fault, it should be for the stew-pot. Forget pedigree when putting the " once-over " on your birds, and don't hesitate much. If the fault is there, well better kill and repent than keep and repent. In the first part you have not really lost anything; in the second, well, your time and money and it possibly takes the place of a really good bird. Now before the babies are twenty-one days old place one or two nest pans with the youngsters in the trap or on the letting board, and watch how they notice the old birds dropping in and out of loft. You cannot start too young! At twenty-one days put them all on the floor of the loft, removing nest pans to the cleaning department for a good washing with soda-water suds,

afterwards drying in the sun with a touch of creosote.
Useful stuff this creosote, keeps all sorts of things away.
Start splashing some of this about when anyone comes
to tell you how to do things and you are in a pensive
mood just picturing to yourself another scoop in the next
race. They go—sure. Keep the youngsters in the old
bird loft for a day or two on the floor. This will clean
up any backward feathers on them ; by huddling together
they get on a heat that breaks the sheaths of any feathers
that are not bursting through quick enough. Do not
worry about them not eating, there is always some old
cock or hen that will feed a crowd of youngsters like this,
and I have even seen other youngsters feeding those not
so lucky as themselves. When weaned take each one for
a final examination before putting in young bird loft, and
do not forget to have your notebook handy. Any faults
will now be easier to find, and don't be sympathetic—they
taste just as nice as a perfect bird. I expect during this
period the novice or beginner is assimilating knowledge
from his loft experiences like a crocodile does food.

CHAPTER V.

HAVING done your job with regard to rearing, your first
round, it is now time to think of training for the races.
If your loft has just been started, take my tip and keep
on breeding one or two real good youngsters and wait
for the young bird racing period, of which I shall speak
later. To the novice who has already birds which have
been previously raced, I address myself, and the system I
am giving is what we call the natural one. The little tips
I shall give you are for the observant fancier who is willing
to take advantage of any little fancies and desires his
pigeons may have. **Individualism stands out, even in a
loft of pigeons.** Watch for this and make notes in your
loft notebook of anything unusual about a bird, then try
to take advantage of same. When you are in the loft, use
your eyes and ears and don't forget to go about with that
bit of seed in your overall pocket, dropping a pinch behind

you now and again. These little things count and all go
to make the birds look up to you as their pal. When one
gets wild and flies about the loft, put it into a nest box and
keep it there until it eats out of your hand, which it will
eventually do. Offer the corn two or three times a day
after the first day. The third is generally sufficient. The
belly tames lions, and at the finish it is kinder to do this
than to kill the bird. A few times in the nest box and you
will have a quieter bird. Most of them will by now be
down again on eggs, which should be removed and re-
placed with dummies. The first part of the training consists of regular exercise, morning and night, and here I
want you to understand the motto of Monsieur Gurnay and
his compere Fred Shaw, late of the Manchester Flying
Club. UP IN THE MORNING IS THE WINNING
GAME, and believe me, it is. Watch how your birds fly
in the early morning air; they get away with a swing and
look as though they were enjoying their job. After the
exercise, be it half-hour or one hour, get them in quickly
and feed a few handfuls of corn, averaging it one quarter
ounce per head, then left quietly together until midday,
when they can again be turned out and fed in with another
quarter of an ounce of the seed mixture. At night, the
exercise should be as late as possible, taking into account
the light. Feed in again with the balance of the corn,
which should average for the day 1-oz. corn mixture and
¼-oz. seed mixture. Please do take notice and believe this
is sufficient for any racing pigeon.

Over-feeding is the bugbear of pigeon racing, and gets
you nowhere, besides being a waste of money. Birds fed
on this system grow in the baskets if they have to be held
up, and do not go sour like over-fed birds who refuse to
feed in the panniers. Keep the exercise up until your
birds are packing well and swinging about like a flock of
starlings. You can then give them a freshener in the
basket for an hour, putting on trough and feeding a little
seed into the panniers, always seeing to it at this stage
that the chippings are fresh and clean. One or two days

of this, then away to a twenty miles toss. This is one of the reasons why I do not wish you to send birds away until they are packing well at home when on the wing. When doing it well you can spring them many miles in their training tosses; in fact, I have often been successful in the first race with pigeons jumped into it without any training toss whatever, but which have flown well around home. Now, twenty miles twice, pick your days, and then forty miles once or twice, after that the first race.

Do not sicken the birds with over-training. If they are flying well around home after the second race they should not require any mid-week toss. Now then, Mr. Working-man, watch this point well. You will find your birds doing as well as the fancier who is basketing and worrying his racers nearly every day. The week before the first race, on the Sunday, give them free hole for an hour or so where possible, and a dose of salts in the drinking water. Fill the bath, outside the loft if at all possible. Monday: Usual exercises and feeding, and if you decide to give a racing or tonic pill, this is the week to do so. Tuesday: Basket the candidates only for the week-end's race and send, weather permissible, the forty or fifty miles toss. Try and arrange for someone—if you cannot be there yourself—to feed them in. A wife interested is worth a great deal, and you should always try, when prize selection comes round at your club, if you have anything to come, to get something useful for her, instead of taking more trouble home with cups and medals. A set of aluminium pans is better with which to get your meals ready—can you hear me, mother? Now to the pigeons again. Wednesday and Thursday: Carry on usual exercise and feed. Friday: **Halt! no exercise, loft, if possible, in partial darkness,** feeding only the quarter ounce seed mixture for breakfast. After that leave birds absolutely alone until basketing time. I do hope you have got your birds coming in to a loud **whistle, bell or rattle.** You will find this very useful on fast days, when they are going over in fours and sixes, racing like Hades. When you see a lot

like this going over, give it 'em good and strong. Many
a good pigeon I have dropped out of the sky with the old
handbell, which would have gone over and away. When
your bird has dropped from the race, do not show any
excitement about the loft ; be calm, do the usual routine
and try to get him quickly amongst the others so as not to
frighten when picking him up. Get the ring off quickly
without dragging the leg, and after ascertaining wing
number put him down gently. Do not be rough or you
may make a bad trapper of the bird. The clock and
thimbles should all be handy and you able to work same
quickly. Rehearse this job of picking a bird up from the
others when they are feeding. Get them used to it.

Having got the races over up to 200 miles, you will have
to alter the training.

CHAPTER VI.

As a beginner, of course, we take it that you will be
having a try at the longer races, this being really a case
of studying individual birds. Some fanciers prefer hens
for long distance racing, but they are harder to get into
condition for a certain day. You have the laying of hens
to watch, and they come into egg at very awkward times.
I have seen as many as ten eggs in the hen panniers when
convoying to the Continental race-points. Taking all
things into consideration, I should say sitting seven or
eight days was the best, or youngsters chipping the eggs,
not hatched out. For cocks, eggs chipping or a youngster
fourteen days old and calling his hen to nest again, but as
I have already said, the fancier will have to look out for
the likes and dislikes of individual birds, if he wishes to be
successful. Exercise should be an hour each morning and
evening, and a loose hour at midday, with bath.

Now here is where you can indulge your birds a little in
the way of feeding. A bit of extra hard flesh will not
come amiss in these long races, but you must not mistake
fat for muscle. When you handle the bird and it feels
heavy and flabby, then it is fat. A bird with the right

kind of weight should handle hard and corky, with soft
silky body feather, and in the case of a cock, strutting
about the loft like a peacock with feathers glistening as
those of that great showy bird. Hens in condition will
usually sit on the nest box perch, tail quivering and eyes
blinking with a great show of watchfulness towards the
nest whilst the cock is sitting. Having seen to it that
they have had the necessary tonic pills during this period,
the birds are now ready for the fray, and you have to trust
them to marking officials and convoyers These people
are mostly efficient and also good fanciers themselves, but
at times a slacker crops up, so it is up to you to keep
your eyes open on marking nights, and anything you see
which you think is a breach of the rules, well, don't forget
to speak out, not for your own sake alone, but for the
other good fanciers **Learn to be alert and fearless, but
not a growler.**

If you have followed out what has been written and
your birds are of a good strain, you should now be getting
results and well up amongst the winners.

We will take it, now that the old bird racing is over,
you are wondering what next to do with your pigeons.
Well, try this. Go through your season's records and
sort out the most consistent cock and hen, pair them
together, and see what kind of a youngster they throw for
you. Of course, do not pair them until they are in good
condition after the racing. This rearing of youngsters
will give them a rest and assist with the moult. You may
get a real good late bred or two which will be very useful
in another twelve months, and if the youngsters are not
the type required, you can separate the pair the following
Spring. I, myself, have bred some very good birds after
racing has finished.

CHAPTER VII.

YOU will now be also training and preparing your
youngsters, and I cannot do better than follow on with
my treatise on

HOW TO WIN YOUNG BIRD RACES.

The fancier has now bred or purchased young birds sufficient for his accommodation or pocket, and I may say at the start that these two points must be strictly watched. Overcrowding means labour lost, and a big loft requires more money to keep up, and what is the use of birds if you cannot afford to enter them in the races.

The successful fancier is the man that likes and feels for his birds, but does not let **sentiment** override him. He must be a kind of sergeant-major as long as the recruits (the young birds) are coming along and trying; well, O.K., but any birds that begin to show a " kink " of any kind, such as wildness, consistent bad trappers, mopsing and diarrhœa after a toss, douse them, get rid.

A good Belgian fancier told me once in a discussion on selection, that most of the successful fanciers in Belgium were ruthless killers in their lofts. They watched very keenly their youngsters in the nest, and any sign of weakness or bad feathering, they killed them, and when they left the nest they were handled, and if not up to the same standard of formation required by him, they went the same way. Better ' kill and repent ' than ' keep and repent,' then you have not wasted time and money.

IMPORTANT.

The novice will, after a time, by concentration on his stud, eventually know what he requires, and then may I ask him to stick to his acquired judgment until he has had reasonable time to prove his stock. Once your stock is proved and you know what you can do with it you must be very careful about any introduction of fresh blood, and if you do introduce something fresh, be sure of its origin, and above all keep a very strict eye on it.

Now for the preparation of the tyros. Loft accommodation, not too much room to fly about in, and ceiling only about six inches over your head. Box perches should

be deep, at least ten inches back to front. This helps you
to handle the birds better; on narrow perches when you
approach them they hop off quickly, on the deep ones they
retire to back of perch, where it is easy to handle them.
With this kind of loft they get used to being handled and
give no trouble at the marking station, causing no rows
between sender and club handler, which does often arise
through no fault of the handler, only he is trying to
subdue a wild youngster. A few loose feathers and heigho
a row and much grumbling, etc.

Now you have selected your youngsters for the racing
(choose only medium or smaller birds, well balanced, apple
bodied youngsters for racing. Large youngsters are
usually too clumsy as tyros). You will take your first nest
birds for the first three races and your second nest birds
for the longer races up to the finish. I have always found
this the best, second nest birds for longer races on account
of these not being so far advanced in the moult as the first
nest. **I mean wing as well as body moult.** Assuming that
you have had the youngsters flying round home well for
a fortnight or more, start the basket training. Putting
the youngsters in the training basket once a day and let
them have a handful of the seed mixture so that they can
rake among the chippings, also put in a water trough after
a day or two. Give them a couple of hours each time, then
liberate near loft, after a week you can take them a mile
away a few times. All this will help to prevent ' flyaways,'
which are all too frequent these days, and to my mind are
the result of letting a batch of highly strung youngsters
have their heads without any home or loft training.

Here at this point I will give you the mixtures of corn
and seed as used by myself with great success :—Corn
Mixture, 40-lbs. good Maples (polished or unpolished) ;
35-lbs. Maize (be sure this is sweet, smell it for sourness),
not too small (Plate Corn or large Galfox Maize if it can
be got is best) ; 15-lbs. Tares (sound), and 15-lbs.
Australian Wheat ; 105-lbs. gross.

BLUE PIED HEN NURP 34 MC 1475.

Bred and Flown by **Mr. C. W. LYONS, Prestwich.**
Winner of **1st PRIZE GUERNSEY, YOUNG BIRD
OPEN RACE,** Manchester F.C. 1934, Velocity 1056,
336 competitors, 1,297 birds.

Also in **Prestwich and District H.S. 2nd Worcestor,
4th Swindon, 1st Bournemouth.**

The Seed Mixture worth its weight in gold. Recipe given in small quantities for the benefit of small lofts. 10-lbs. Black Rape, 5-lbs. White Millet, 5-lbs. Hempseed, 2½-lbs. Canary Seed, 2½-lbs. Linseed, 5-lbs. Groats, 2-lbs. Rice—32-lbs. gross.

The feed per day per head is One Ounce of Corn Mixture and a Quarter Ounce of Seed Mixture given as follows :—Half-ounce of corn mixture after morning exercise and the quarter-ounce seed mixture in the early afternoon, or coming in from training toss, and balance of corn after last fly at night. Do not give your birds free hole, it makes them into bad trappers. Make them at home inside the loft, and do not make any violent noises inside or outside of loft, but do not creep about, go about in your natural way.

Do not let anyone come into loft with a **bowler hat on,** he is sure to knock it off, and then you will know what has happened ; frightens them worse than a cat. Don't wear spectacles in or about the loft on race days or allow anybody else. The flashing of the glasses as you move about startles your racer and unnerves it. Do not look a bird in the eye when trapping, it will cause him to hesitate, but above all, when amongst your birds, be your natural self ; they will always know you by your ways and settle accordingly. Do not let birds out until you have cleaned the loft out ; this gets them used to you and your noise as much as anything.

Now, having got so far, we will start the youngsters on to the proper training stages. We will start at five miles about four times, picking the days if possible. Always have someone to trap in with the seed mixture ; late arrivals get nothing until evening feed, also those that stay on top of loft the same treatment. From five to fifteen miles a few times, then to thirty miles a couple of times, and on to about fifty miles, this being the last training point, and as many times as possible ; always keep freshening up their memories with this toss, having had a good grounding up to this point they will be hard to lose. Now during all these tosses you should have been keeping your eyes open and making notes of any outstanding birds for the earlier races. Bear in mind little plums are very sweet and help to pay the corn bill.

The week before the first race you have selected a team, the number according to your means. You have selected birds showing sensibility about the loft, consistency in the training tosses, and birds that have flown well around home.

Each night during that week you will give them **Two Racing Pills,** and if weather inclined to be sunless and cold give **One H.L.O. Capsule also each night.** One toss on Tuesday or Wednesday, not later. **Friday breakfast, only ¼-oz. of Seed Mixture,** and they must not be let out for exercise on that day ; in fact keep out of loft yourself until basketing time, and if it is possible to darken loft that day do so.

Further to the above a few general hints, which should be keenly watched. Do not have rock salt lying about the loft, it gathers all the dust, and your birds get this when they lick the salt and it does not satisfy. The better way and most sanitary is to put a tablespoonful of salt into a gallon of the drinking water during the breeding time each day and once or twice a week during racing. **Do not put large quantities of grit** before your birds, it is liable to become fouled. Re-fill grit pots three or four times a week. There are so many good grits on the market that it would be hard to say which I prefer ; a hard limestone slightly salted by myself, or break up finely an old rustic blue brick—this is fine as a grit.

Green Food.—You cannot beat watercress or dandelion, when not procurable a cabbage cut into halves, slightly salted, and above all else **do not overfeed.**

Birds do not grow with overfeeding, they mope and laze about. Give them the required allowance as stated, then you will see them grow and become alert and active. What looks worse than corn lying about in a loft and becoming fouled? You cannot condition pigeons under these conditions. Clean out once a day, the morning preferred, as early as possible, and then get the birds out and on the wing. Don't let any backward youngsters lie about the top loft. **On the wing or in the loft** should be the motto, with the exception of the day after the race, when you can let them out for an hour or so and the bath. If your birds are troubled with feather lice, make up a not too strong lotion of Izal; get a rose tree spray and a friend to open the bird's wings, then spray well under wings and the rump feathers, also back of neck, keeping fingers and thumb over the eyes during this part of the operation; once in the season is usually enough. Pick a sunny day for this and place birds on top of loft as you do them. Never let youngsters out with a full crop. A handful of toasted breadcrumbs flavoured with a little salt first thing in the morning before going out for exercise do not come amiss to either old or young birds. Follow out these instructions or as near as possible to your circumstances, and you cannot help but be amongst the prize-winners.

A few after-thoughts and additions:—Never send youngsters to training toss without having first given them a few lessons in the basket. This does avoid losses caused through what is termed " basket fright " at time of liberation.

When calling birds into loft either by word, bell, whistle or rattle, give them plenty of it during feeding time only, and never call them unless you have some corn or tit-bit to give them.

When you notice a couple of youngsters pairing up in the loft, don't separate them, but make the best out of this state. Place a nest pan in corner of loft floor, and when they have taken to it and so as not to allow the young hen to get into " egg," place a couple of dummy eggs in the nest, one at a time. This will usually satisfy them, and they will sit on indefinitely. On basketing day for the race, slip a baby youngster in the nest two or three hours before basketing ; see that they both have a turn with the baby. I have put up some real good performances when I have had youngsters in this state. When they return from the race do not put the youngster back, but let them carry on with the eggs and repeat the following week with the baby.

If by any chance one of the old cocks takes a fancy to a young hen and she follows him into the old bird loft, well, make the most of it, but do not leave her with him during the night, an hour or two during the day only. On basketing day for race keep her away from him until basketing time, then slip her into the old bird loft, having previously put another hen in to the cock. Give her two or three minutes looking through the bars at him, and then put her into the basket and do not forget to pool her.

Keep a sharp look-out for any little fancies your birds may have and make the best of them.

Trapping.—If you have to have a trap and not able to use the open door, be sure it is simple and not one of the " Harry Tate " sort. In place of a trap I prefer a " let " board level inside and outside of loft, with a row of light-weight bolting wires to run through. If a bird has to drop into the loft let him do it when he is safe through the wires ; if he has to drop through drop holes into a trap or even the loft, they oftener than not hesitate and sometimes long enough to lose the race for you, especially if birds have been on wing some time, and after having their legs tucked up behind them for hours, they do not feel like taking the drop into loft, but will certainly go through wires on seeing their loft mates feeding level on the inside.

The Wing Moult.—Do not allow this to worry you during the racing period as long as nature is taking its pre-ordained course, that is one feather well up before casting the next one.

You will hear fanciers and writers say that casting of a feather causes pain and leaves the wing sore. Don't you believe it. Nature does not allow its subjects to be constantly in pain because it is going through the course of re-feathering as ordained by nature itself. Carry on, unless you have a subject that has cast two feathers together; then you can with every confidence rest this bird a week or two.

Last of all, do not let **sentiment** over-ride your better judgment with your pigeons, and do not let your loft get over-stocked with old pensioners. Get rid of them ; your employer will get rid of you when you are non-productive.

So good luck and good flying weather to you all.

Pigeon Foods and Mixtures.—In the first place I am not going to write round about on this subject, but to plump right away for grain of all sorts to be no more than one year old and **unpolished.** Sound, well harvested grain of any kind **does not** require polishing. A good racing mixture may be made up as follows for old birds (the grain to be not more than twelve months old, unpolished) :—Maples, 28-lbs. : small tics, 14-lbs. ; plate maize (medium), 42-lbs. ; good tares (not necessarily the largest), 14-lbs. ; wheat (bold), 14-lbs. You can race anywhere on this mixture, and it is not expensive. If good tares are not available, use lentils ; these are just as good and usually cheaper. If tares are good and cheaper than maples, cut out some maples and add the equivalent in tares. Seed mixture which is worth its weight in gold to a keen fancier : Black rape seed (colza), 10-lbs. ; white millett, 5-lbs. ; hemp seed, 5-lbs. ; canary seed, 2½-lbs. ; linseed, 2½-lbs. ; groats, 5-lbs. ; rice, 2-lbs. ; total, 32-lbs.

The Mixture for the Moult.

Plate Maize	30%	Linseed	5%
Sunflower Seed... ...	20%	Lentils	5%
Tics and Maples ...	10%	Tares	5%
Barley	5%	Rape Seed (Colza) ...	10%
New Wheat	10%		

A little buckwheat or dari, if good, can be added. Feed twice daily until moult finished and keep loft warm at night.

Corn Bins.—Store your corn in a well-ventilated box, and on no account in a metal bin, which makes it sweat. The box bottom should be made of perforated zinc or gauze; also the lid. Move the box once or twice a week to disturb the corn. Your corn will always be sweet in one of these receptacles. Then there is the revolving drum with six compartments. The drum is hexagon-shaped, the doors made with fine gauze in a wood frame, a sliding bar fastening them into position. The whole stands on a pair of supported legs like a windlass. Should you wish to store the winter's feed, and unfortunately have only an outshed near the loft to do this, you must see to it that the roof is in good condition and the floor boarded. If the floor is of concrete, put down a wooden stillage, with two or three handfuls of powdered lime to each hundred-weight of corn. This will keep away mildew and weevils, and does the corn no harm nor the birds, and what a lovely colour your beans or peas will be the following Spring. Make sure your store-room is free from rats or mice. If this cannot be done you had better buy the corn as required.

Grit.—I favour a good hard limestone grit or one or two of the old rustic blue bricks put through the grit smasher. Re-fill grit pots two or three times per week; don't let grit get dusty and fouled.

Salt.—Do not use rock salt or lickers. Dust is attracted, and getting tainted with the salt the birds eat

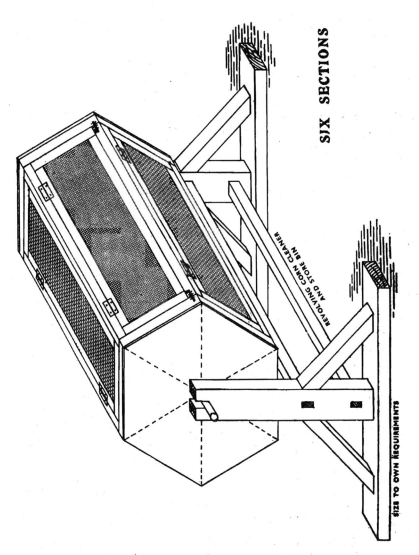

SIX SECTIONS

REVOLVING CORN CLEANER

READ AND STORE BIN

SIZE TO OWN REQUIREMENTS

SKETCH OF CORN BIN.

it eagerly. Then your trouble begins. Use table salt when necessary in the water, once a week in the winter, when feeding youngsters every day.

FOREWORD TO MY ACCOUNT OF MY BELGIUM VISIT.

I do not wish fanciers to think for one moment that I am trying to give out the impression that the Belgian racers are superior to our own birds. Not at all. In all countries you have to take the geographical route the birds have to fly. I will name four routes; I will put what I call the easiest first and the hardest of all the last. First we have the Belgium route; no water to cross, and finish up in what you might term a flat country. The Belgians specialise in races 100 to 200 miles, and they get plenty of sport from this class of racing, some districts flying these distances all the year round. They give more prizes in their races than we do; usually one prize for every ten entrants. If you wish to win big money in the races you have to put big money down. The odds you would pick up, if a winner, would be about 3's or 5's to 1. The prizes are well spread out. This, to me, is as it should be.

The second route on the list is the English North Road; the third the English South Road to France, and beyond. The water jump is where many birds fail. And the last and hardest route known for a racing pigeon is the North of Ireland route, where the pigeons have to finish most of the journey over sea and mountains. I might mention the route to Scotland is also very formidable racing from France.

In giving these routes you will see where the super pigeon is required. One of bulldog tenacity and the will to carry on and a fancier behind it with that 50 per cent. knowledge of his subject.

The old pioneers of long distance pigeon racing, almost all of them, have crossed the " Great Divide," had greater difficulties to overcome than what we to-day have to face,

and it would take a very large book and an abler pen than
mine to do them justice.   These fanciers spared neither
time nor money in going about home or abroad to find the
best of racing pigeon blood, and the result of their untiring
efforts shows in the strains of English racing pigeons,
which are second to none in the world.   Down the South
of England, J. W. Logan, Esq., A. H. Osman, Esq.,
editor of " The Racing Pigeon," Harrison, and many
others.   In Lancashire here we had the late Ted Burrows,
Esq., John Webster, Esq., and J. Toft, Esq., and scores
of others.   Our pioneer fanciers of the old days must
have been real men and very keen to carry on like they did
with all the prejudice of the public up against pigeon flyers.

Here's to those pioneer fanciers !   May their memories
ever be kept green !

BELGIUM AND SOME LOFTS.

During my recent visit to Belgium (August, 1937) I
inspected several of the most famous lofts, and will
describe them without mentioning these fanciers' names
but by giving details of the systems of racing their birds.

The first loft I visited was in company with that great
London fancier and sportsman, Alfred R. Hancock, of
Woolwich; also our old and invaluable Belgian friend,
Jules L. Maesenaere, of Zarren, a wonderful guide and
interpreter.   What could we do without him ?   The British
fancier owes a lot to my friend Jules in various ways.
The loft was that owned by Mynheer " A," of Moere, who
showed us a wonderful team of birds.   The origin of them
were the Wegges from the old Padre Wegge, brother of
the famous Charles Wegge.   There were several outstanding racers that had put up most unique performances in
the Western section of Flanders and in the long distance
competitions.   The system of widowhood is practised for
the long races as well as the short.   I have seen a good
deal of so-called widowhood systems in England, but until
then I had never had the chance of having the system

explained to me by four of Belgium's leading aces. The systems as practised by these fanciers must have a chapter to themselves.

M. " A.'s " feeding was such that over here we would say it was almost impossible for birds to perform consistently on such food. The mixture he used, of which I have a sample, contains : 60 per cent. good sound plate maize ; 20 per cent. really good tics (last season's) ; 15 per cent. good grey tares ; 5 per cent. bold wheat, all of real good quality and only one season old. It is unpolished but riddled in the bins. I may point out that not one of all the fanciers in Belgium would have polished corn. M " A. " uses a seed mixture similar to M. He showed me innumerable special prizes until I was quite bewildered. I lost some of M. " A.'s " notes, but it is really this corn and system work I wish to write about in this little book of mine. I have samples of these mixtures which I shall be pleased to show anyone interested. I am sure if any of the British corn merchants would take up and put them on the market at the right price they would be doing the working man fancier a good turn by bringing more members into the sport and making more business. What should it matter to a corn merchant if he sells one cwt. of maize instead of one cwt. of maples, if he gets the same profit? Why does any article require polishing?˙ It must be old, dirty, or in the case of grain, perhaps musty. New sound corn requires no polishing, the riddle will do all that is necessary. I told you at the beginning of this book that I was no " Blatchford " or Dr. Barker as a writer, but this corn business does really get me wound up, and has done so for years.

On leaving M. " A.'s," a visit was paid to M. " B.'s " place at Oudeport. He is a nurseryman and horticulturist. M. " B. " flies some grand pigeons, and his performances in the international races this last few years are astonishing. The family of birds consists of descendants of pigeons he bought direct from Dr. Bricoux, of Jollimont, with a later introduction of the Bekeman Wegges.

They are a typical colony of fine outstanding blues with
good broad bars, blue chequers with here and there white
flights; also a few pied headed ones. M. " B." does
not fly young birds, and trains only the yearlings. When
two years old they go anywhere. Now you can understand why his birds appear large and when handled the
bone structure feels like steel girders. He also flies on
the widowhood system, and from Pau, Bordeaux, and
other long distances, he is the " untouchable " of
Belgium. Cups and medals galore. He won this year
the " Le Soir " Cup. The " Le Soir " is a newspaper
of large circulation. They presented a handsome trophy
nineteen years ago, and put 500 francs into the cup each
year to be won outright. It had to be won twice in
succession in the international, which was thought to be
practically impossible, but M. " B." has done it. I saw
his feeding and had his system explained. What birds!
When you handle them and shut your eyes you would
think you were in a pigeon heaven, if there is such a place.
Anyhow, I have a list here of his winnings that will tell
you more than I can.

M. " B." won since 1929, 90 prizes in the National Pau
Race, including one first and four seconds. Distance from
Pau to Oudeport, West Flanders, 930 kilometres. Yearly
results in this great race:—

1929. Open 2nd, 12th, 17th, 23rd, and 58th.

1929. Western Section 1st winner of the Grand Silver
Cup which the " Le Soir " presents for the best two
nominated birds. The Cup to be won outright by the
competitor winning it twice in succession, and each year
500 francs is added until Cup is won outright. Winner
takes the lot.

1930 (1,082 birds competing). 42nd, 97th, and 3 other
prizes.

1931 (1,196 birds competing). 2nd, 26th, 34th, and 4
others. Western Section 1st and 11th.

1932 (2,998 birds competing). 2nd, 6th, 12th, 14th, 15th, and 10 other prizes. Winner of Special Prize given by Mons. Jules Janssens and 3 other Grand Specials.

1933 (3,341 birds competing). 21st, 79th, 180th, and 11 other positions.

1934 (2,607 birds competing). 53rd, 60th, and 6 other prizes. Western Section, 3rd, 4th, 23rd, and 4 other prizes.

1935 (2,002 birds competing). 1st, 14th, 46th, and 10 other prizes. Western Section, 1st, 3rd, 5th, 12th, 17th, 18th, 21st, and 29th.

1936 (1,814 birds competing), 12th, 14th, 24th, and 6 other prizes. Won outright the " Le Soir " Cup, which contained 4,500 francs. Western Section, 1st, 2nd, 3rd, and 3 other prizes.

1937 (1,210 birds competing). 2nd, 24th, 26th, and 9 other prizes. Winning the new " Le Soir " Cup and also the King Leopold's Gold Bracelet Watch Special.

This list of M. " B." is given to you really to show that it is not necessary to pay big prices for old peas and corn to get results. Good sound year-old grain is all that is required. M. " B." also wins in the short and middle distances.

The next visit we paid was to one of Belgium's wonder-ful lofts overlooking the City of Brussels. M. " C.," the man that can christen his pigeons all sorts of fancy and weird names, which he remembers quite well. M. " C." was kindness itself. When we had regaled ourselves with a bottle of beer (Alf. was not on beer, only Jules and I), we went up to the loft at the top of the refreshment build-ing situated in one of Brussels' glorious parks. When you look round from the roof and see miles upon miles of good, flat country, you ask yourself is it the man or the birds? This question I asked M. " C." before we left, and here is his answer. " Well," my friend, I think it is what you call fifty-fifty. But if a man has a good bird which only gets what you might say ordinary care, and

comes along and wins, I should give the bird 90 marks
and owner 10, and vice-versa.   However good the pigeon
is it cannot win unless it is sent away in winning condition, and that, my friend, is for each and every fancier
to find out for himself when his birds are in their best
condition and in what they fly their best, too.   We
handled, many of M. " C.'s " champions or aces as they
called them.   " KOHINOOR," his greatest winner, and
" Kohinoor's " hen, " KALOMEA," he would not take
£1,000 for.   They were great to handle, and had won at
all distances.   We also examined " KIRGHIZ," another
big prize-winning pigeon and a perfect bird, also
" LACOUSTIC " and many others that had won well
and were a treat to handle.   M. " C." stated that most of
his " aces " had known 400 miles as young birds. Feeding
does not cost so much there as we pay here, as they cut out
a lot of the heavy corn such as maples and tics, though
tics are mostly in use in preference to maples, which are
too expensive in comparison to their feeding value against
tic beans.   They give their pigeons more variety in the
diet than we British fanciers do.   If a pigeon is very fond
of a certain kind of grain and is doing well on it, why take
it away from him?   They say if he is eating coal and
flying and well on it, then give him more coal.   We are
too orthodox in the way of feeding pigeons.   When the
late great Vandenbusche, of Brussels, was at his zenith,
he showed me a biscuit tin that he kept in the oven, and
into which all the household crusts from the loaves of
bread went.   When nicely toasted, they were smashed up
in a cloth bag, salted a little and fed to the birds in the
morning before their first exercise.   He said to me in his
quaint way, " Fly well, belly not too empty this morning."
And they did fly, believe me.   I saw them several times
fly over the city warehouses, etc., for an hour and a half.
He put this down to the breadcrumbs before turning out
in the morning.   So you see, working men fanciers, there
are many ways of economising on the corn bill.   I myself
have used blue, grey, and so-called white peas, also the
marrowfat peas, with real good results.   Why should we

nor use whichever is the cheapest? The dietetic analysis
is practically the same. I have heard fanciers say their
birds won't eat this and that. It is because this certain
thing has been put into the mixture which they have not
been used to. Always feed any fresh kind of grain to the
pigeons separately, and some time before they get the
bulk. They soon come to eat it in the mixture when this
is done.

Now back to the loft of another great Brussels fancier,
M. " D." It is quite a coincidence that he flies the old
Goossen strain of birds. He is a very keen fancier with
a fine set of lofts overlooking the aerodrome at Brussels.
M. " D." flies both the widowhood and the natural
systems, the latter, he says, being to pick out the good
hens for his best cocks, for reproduction. In-breeding, but
not too close. This is a point about which I wish to write
while it is in my mind. When you are in Belgium and talk
of pedigree, you never hear the dam's side much discussed.
The Belgian fancier purchasing a bird, say a descendant
of some famous cock, would take it for granted that this
famous cock would only have the best hen in the loft
paired to him.

Pedigree, unless containing winning strains in the last
two or three generations, is not of much use. The bird
should be good to handle, and its sire or dam, grandsire or
grand-dam should have had " winning ways " on many
days. I have seen a bird's pedigree advertised in England
in a sale advertisement, which cost twenty-seven shillings.
What is the use of pedigree unless it is backed up by
performances as previously stated. During the last two
or three seasons, in Brussels, fanciers there say that it has
been all M. " D." in the races. His pigeons are a treat
to handle. He has an old loft man, but also a son about
seventeen who is very keen and enthusiastic. M. " D."
has the birds, the position, and all the help necessary,
together with the £ s. d. ; also the keenness and desire to
win to carry him successfully for a good many years in
the pigeon racing sport. He feeds separate grain and

also a mixture similar to the Stassart regime, but is also very fond of good maize when it can be found. It was a great pleasure to be in the company of such a fancier; in fact, when we had to leave him my eyes filled with tears so that I could hardly see him. No, I was not drunk, just reluctant to part from a good fancier so soon.

Our visit to M. " E.," of Liege, will live in my mind for ever. What pigeons, and the type, many fanciers would say he could hardly help himself but win; but not so M. " E.," who says however good your birds are you must do your share of the job to send them away in perfect condition. Could I chance my money on ill-conditioned birds? He says he cannot always win, but is quite satisfied to know the bird went away in FORM. M. " E." gave me a very good reason why he preferred the widowhood system for the long races. The pigeon flying on that system is quieter and calmer in the basket, accustomed to being fastened up in the box in the loft, and therefore does not worry or knock itself about. He says watch the bird flying on the natural system, in the basket. It never seems to settle down, and if it has left a youngster behind will naturally fill itself up with corn which it cannot get rid of, with the possibility of turning sour. The bird is then finished so far as that race is concerned. Always conserve the energy of your birds, exercise at regular times, then quietness and rest in their own boxes when the loft is in semi-darkness.

THE WIDOWHOOD SYSTEM.
As Practised by M. " E.," Liege.

Now M. " E." is a believer of studying his birds individually, and as such it causes him to make little alterations in the system to suit different types.

The nest boxes for the widowhood system comprises two compartments of equal size, and the length is just double the depth from front to back. .This is so that one of the front halves, which are hinged in the centre, can be folded back to enable the hen to be fastened up without

the cock coming into contact with her. They are thus
able to bill and coo and do everything bar the extreme.
M. " E." allows the pairs to sit only from six to ten days
before taking the hen and eggs away. In the case of a
cock that has been a bit slow with his moult the previous
season, he would allow that cock to rear a youngster to
ten days old before taking away. This, he says, would
give him a good start for the season's moult. Having
taken the hens away, the loft is taboo to all strangers, and
until racing is over only he and his loftman enter it. The
cocks are not even allowed to fly about the loft; they
are fastened up in the nest box, fed and watered in same,
and only allowed out of it for flying exercise. When the
hens have been moved out of sight and sound of the loft,
they are kept in separate boxes, because if not they would
pair together and lay, which naturally would defeat the
whole object of the system. Once or twice during the
week the hens are put back into the boxes ready for when
the cocks re-enter from exercise. The cocks cannot reach
the hens, and after about an hour the hens are taken away
and the loft, by arrangement of shutters or blinds, put into
semi-darkness. You will have to be prepared to waste a
little corn during this system, because the biggest job is
to get the cocks to feed during this treatment, and that is
why a mixture is used which they like. If you notice a
bird relishing some particular grain, then see to it having
plenty of that grain in the feed. The birds are exercised
three times per day, the first as early possible in the
morning, afterwards feeding with the seed mixture. Be
sure that the birds go right to their boxes on entering.
After a few days there is very little trouble. The training
is not done in big jumps, but short tosses are necessary.
The hen is always in the box on the cock's arrival. He is
allowed to be with her for a few minutes, though on no
consideration must he tread the hen, but be taken away
when she is getting too keen. Carry on with this treatment of training, always choosing good days, if possible.
Birds that are not eating too well, see they have good
racing or tonic pills the week before going away. On

return from the race the cock is allowed his hen for a couple of hours, also the bath and whatever they like to eat. Then the hen goes away again until the mid-week, when the cock can see her again following the return from the training toss. Handle the birds pretty often, and see that they are keeping their weight, making sure that the boxes are kept very clean. Always carry a little cane into the loft, and if the birds are getting too noisy draw it ʻacross the bars on the box fronts sharply to stop them. Only let them on the loft floor a few minutes together for a spot of seed prior to going out for exercise. Leave the birds to themselves as much as possible, and make sure the nest boxes are properly fastened, because if they ever get together it means murder. After the morning exercise feed with a seed mixture, and at mid-day give them a light feed with a seed mixture, while in the evening feed with tics, maples, tares, maize, lentils. Put salt in water once a week. This system is carried out by Mons. " B.," only that he allows all the birds to sit at the beginning six to eight days. He does not feed with a mixture, but finds out what the individual birds like, and feeds accordingly, using judgment in the matter.

Mons. " C." and Mynheer " A." let each pair rear the first round, while Mons. " D." follows out the same as Mons. " E.," who studies individualism. Mons. " C.," of course, races young birds up to 400 miles, but does not fly them as yearlings.

THE " JEALOUSY " SYSTEM.

Mons. " E." had a nice team of youngsters for the races. He has what is called a jealousy system, employing this on one or two early young cocks and some of the yearlings. It is a three-compartment box with dowelled partitions. Two young cocks of the same colour are paired to one old hen. The hen is then put into the centre compartment of the box and a young cock is placed on each side of her. By this arrangement the hen does plenty of bowing and scraping from one cock to the other, causing the green-eyed monster of jealousy to grow in the hearts of the young cocks. Now and then the sliding partition is drawn out for one of the cocks to be with the hen for a few minutes, but always keeping a watchful eye on them to see that no treading takes place. The next thing to do is to replace the partition, giving the other cock a chance, and so on during exercise and training. On basketing day, the birds are out for a short exercise, and as they re-enter the loft find the old cock, which the hen had previously been paired to, in with her. After viewing this for a minute or two, the young cocks are put into the basket ready for the clubhouse. Of course, you will have to see to it that the youngsters have not been neglecting themselves with the feeding, and above all see they have a good tonic or racing pill a few days before the race. This will stop them from going stale.

The Pigeon Auction Sales

THE beginner or novice should certainly attend all the Pigeon Auction Sales that are held within his reach. He will learn more at one of these sales in one afternoon than he would visiting lofts for twelve months.

First of all he would get to know the types of the different strains that are offered from time to time, and also the strains kept by many successful fanciers who make use of the Auction Sale for disposal of their surplus stock. You will come in contact with good fanciers who are always ready to help the beginner. Don't be afraid to ask them any questions you have in mind. They are a sporting lot, these pigeon fanciers. The Auction Sales are the stamping ground of a great many old fanciers who like to meet one another and talk of the pigeon racing events, and a lot of this talk is very entertaining and you will pick up many good tips. So look out for the Auction Sale adverts. when the season commences.

Lightning Source UK Ltd.
Milton Keynes UK
02 April 2011

170281UK00001B/135/P